LOVE TO LANGSTON

by TONY MEDINA

illustrated by R. GREGORY CHRISTIE

Lee & Low Books Inc.

New York

For my cousins who grew up with me—
Steven, Kathy, Ralph, Desiree, and Jenevie.
And to the memory of Raymond R. Patterson,
master poet and heir to Langston's blues aesthetic
    —T.M.

For Jamal and Leon Jackson,
two great allies during my own "first grade" days
    —R.G.C.

Text copyright © 2002 by Tony Medina
Illustrations copyright © 2002 by R. Gregory Christie

Printed in Hong Kong by South China Printing Co. (1988) Ltd.

Book design by Christy Hale
Book production by The Kids at Our House

The text is set in American Gothic
The illustrations are rendered in acrylics
Back cover photograph by Griffith J. Davis, from the Yale Collection
of American Literature, Beinecke Rare Book and Manuscript Library.
Reprinted by permission of Harold Ober Associates Incorporated.

10 9 8 7 6 5 4 3 2 1
First Edition

Library of Congress Cataloging-in-Publication Data
Medina, Tony.
Love to Langston / by Tony Medina ; illustrated by R. Gregory Christie.— 1st ed.
p. cm.
Summary: A series of poems written from the point of view of the poet Langston Hughes,
offering an overview of key events and themes in his life.
ISBN 1-58430-041-8
1. Hughes, Langston, 1902–1967—Juvenile poetry. 2. African American poets—Juvenile poetry.
3. Children's poetry, American. 4. Poets—Juvenile poetry. [1. Hughes, Langston, 1902–1967—
Poetry. 2. Poets, American—Poetry. 3. African Americans—Poetry. 4. American poetry.]
I. Christie, R. Gregory, 1971– ill. II. Title.
PS3563.E2414 L68 2002   811'.54—dc21   2001038140

The author and publisher would like to thank Dr. Jonathan Scott, Professor of English, City University
of New York, for his help with the preparation of this book.

Sources

Berry, Faith. *Langston Hughes: Before and Beyond Harlem*. Westport, CT: Lawrence Hill, 1983.
Hill, Christine M. *Langston Hughes: Poet of the Harlem Renaissance*. Springfield, NJ: Enslow, 1997.
Hughes, Langston. *The Big Sea: An Autobiography*. New York: Thunder's Mouth, 1986.
——. *The Dream Keeper and Other Poems*. New York: Knopf, 1932.
——. *Langston Hughes Reads His Poetry, with Commentary and Reflections from the Author*. New York:
    Caedmon, 1980. (audiocassette)
——. *Selected Poems*. New York: Vintage, 1974.
Osofsky, Audrey. *Free to Dream: The Making of a Poet: Langston Hughes*. New York: Lothrop, Lee &
    Shepard, 1996.
Rampersad, Arnold. *The Life of Langston Hughes, Volume I: 1902–1941, I Too Sing America*. New York
    and Oxford: Oxford University Press, 1986.
——. *The Life of Langston Hughes, Volume II: 1941–1967, I Dream a World*. New York and Oxford:
    Oxford University Press, 1988.
Rummel, Jack. *Langston Hughes: Poet*. New York: Chelsea House, 1988.
St. Claire-borne. *Voices & Visions*. "Langston Hughes: The Dream Keeper." New York: New York Center
    for Visual History, 1988. (videocassette)
Walker, Alice. *Langston Hughes, American Poet*. New York: Thomas Y. Crowell, 1974.

LANGSTON HUGHES' *Selected Poems* was one of the first poetry books I ever read. The cover had a photo of Langston sitting in front of his typewriter, looking over his shoulder with a slight, hesitating grin. It was the first brown face I had ever seen looking out at me from the cover of a book—a face that reminded me of *my* face and the faces of my family.

When I opened the book, a whole world of familiar voices and scenes came to life. Langston was painting my world with words both plainspoken and lyrically sweet and sassy. Langston's Harlem was the Harlem of my father and grandmother, of my aunts and uncles. It was the first time poetry truly spoke to me about where I was from, in language that was familiar, reminding me of the people in my neighborhood.

I went on to read more books by Langston and books written about him. I learned how important he was to American literature in general and black literature in particular. A poet of the people, Langston celebrated the beauty of black life, and his poetry, plays, and short stories expressed his lifelong commitment to justice and equality. Langston was one of the first poets to read his poetry to jazz and to integrate jazz and the blues into his own poems. He was immediately embraced because his work was accessible and every word expressed his deep love of the people. This is the Langston I wish for you to meet in this book, which represents one Harlem poet's homage to another.

Love to Langston captures glimpses of Langston's life in the art form he cherished most—poetry. It is an introduction to Langston's world through his voice as I would imagine it, so that he comes to life speaking to you from yesterday and today, in the here and now. At the back of the book, notes provide a broader biographical context for the poems and Langston's life.

—Tony Medina
Harlem, USA

Little Boy
Blues

Little boy little boy
little boy blues
why can't I go out
to play too
little boy blues

Little boy little boy
little boy blues
reading and dreaming
and watching Grandma
snooze

The white kids chase me
'cause of the color of
my skin
said the white kids chase me
'cause of my brown brown skin

Little boy little boy
little boy blues
where's Mama at
and Papa at
little boy blues

Why can't I go out
to play too
little boy blues

Grandma's
Stories

Grandma has a head full of stories
she has a whole heart full of stories

All day long when Mama's away
Grandma wraps me in her special shawl
and tells me her stories

Black people stolen from Africa into slavery
black people with no rights working for free

Black slaves who escaped on the Underground Railroad
not a choo-choo train with a running engine
but black folks and white folks working together
to bring slaves from the South up North to freedom

Grandma fills me full of stories
she thrills me with her stories

Of how she is African, French and Cherokee
and how they tried to kidnap her into slavery

Grandma tells me her stories wrapped in her shawl
that has its own story with its bloodstains and
bullet holes and all from her husband who was
killed with John Brown at Harpers Ferry

Oh, I know Grandma's stories are true
they didn't come from school or any book
Grandma was there fighting for freedom too!

First
Grade

In Topeka, Kansas
the teacher makes me sit
in the corner
in the last row
far away from
the other kids

She rolls her eyes
and sucks her teeth
with heavy heavy sighs
and lies and lies

She tells one kid
not to eat licorice
or he'll turn black
      like me

When Mama finds out
she takes me out of school
she rolls her eyes
and sucks her teeth
with heavy heavy sighs

And why why why

Jim Crow
Row

In the seventh grade
in Lawrence, Kansas
the teacher puts all
us black kids in the same row
away from all the white kids

I don't roll my eyes
or suck my teeth
with a heavy heavy sigh
and a why why why

I make signs
that read
that read

Jim Crow Row
Jim Crow Row
we in the Jim Crow Row

Jim Crow is a law
that separates white and black
making white feel better
and black feel left back

So we protest
with our parents
and let everybody
know about

Jim Crow Jim Crow
not allowing us
to grow

Jim Crow Jim Crow
don't put us in a
Jim Crow Row

Libraries

Libraries
are a special place
for me

with their long tables
all smooth and shiny
and bookcases spilling

      over

with books filled with
wonderful worlds

Libraries
are a special place
for me

to sit and to stay
with books and books
and books of endless

beautiful words

keeping me company
taking my loneliness
and blues

      away

In
High School

I live in a white neighborhood
go to a white school, but I don't feel
out of place, I feel like I have found a home

My friends are white but outsiders like me
'cause their parents are immigrants from Russia
Poland, Italy and Hungary

I run track, do the high jump, join the relay
team, act in the school play, write poems
and stories for the school magazine—
I'm a scream!

But I have to grow up fast 'cause Mama
wants me to quit school and work

It doesn't make any sense to me
how could I get a job without a degree
I have to make a tough decision
to work at sixteen would be a prison

I take an attic room in Cleveland
eat hot dogs and sticky rice each night
trying not to freeze while I study
work on my poems and read myself to sleep

I have some high times and low times
some fast times and slow times
some real stop-and-go times—
it's my I'm-running-out-of-time-
to-be-a-kid-gotta-grow time!

I Do Not Like
My Father Much

I do not like my father much
he is selfish and angry and
calls black people such-and-such

I do not like what he has to say
that writing poems for a living
will not pay

I do not like what my father wants
me to be, a miner of silver in Mexico
a graduate with an engineering degree

I want to be my own man
go to Harlem and become a poet
for black people and poor people
those my father calls such-and-such

In Harlem I send him a letter
choosing poetry over college
he chooses to do me one better
never sending me another letter

My father is a man who could not do what
he wanted to do or be what he wanted to be
so he takes out his pain on everyone
even his own family

His anger causes me pain
just the same

No, I do not like my father much

Leaving Harlem
for Africa

Leaving Harlem for Africa
in search of myself
I throw my books over the ship
into the black mouth of the sea

The water must be hungry
'cause it swallows
those books down mean

I am letting go of my past
like tears dropped from my face
one by one

Books I read as a lonely lonely child
books I hardly read at college
uptown in Harlem running wild

I want to change myself and grow
set out on my own journey
nothing left but my
imagination and memory

Learn from experience
not just books

Leaving Harlem for Africa
I stare at the mouth
of the great big sea
swallowing my books

Glad it ain't me

All My
Life

I travel the big seas
working on ships to pay my fee
countries and continents welcome me

In Paris, in Africa, Russia and China
I go around the world like a miner
not the kind my father wants me to be
in Mexico with an engineering degree

But a miner searching for riches
from people of all races
discovering other voices and places

Going around the world claiming poets
from other nations, translating their sonnets
and stories into something I can dig—
yeah, going around the world digging life is my gig!

When I'm not overseas I'm in Harlem
with writers, artists and musicians
mapping out a world of laughter and strife
celebrating the beauty of black life

Harlem Is the
Capital of My World

Harlem is the capital of my world
black and beautiful and bruised
like me

Harlem has soul—it's where black people
care about black people and everybody's
child belongs to the community

Where we be stylin' and profilin'
with concrete streets stretched out
under our feet and boulevards broad
and spread like a red carpet for royalty

The King of Swing
The Duke of Ellington
The Empress of the Blues

Harlem is a bouquet of black roses
all packed together and protected
by blackness and pride

Harlem is where I reside
where I work and stride
my dark community
from the East River to
St. Nicholas Avenue with
nightclubs and cabarets
spilling over with jazz
and bluesy urban spirituals
(it's no miracle we survive!)

Why I fell in love with Harlem
before I ever got here!

Yeah, Harlem is where I be—
where I could be
Me

Harlem is the capital of my world

Jazz
Makes Me Sing

Jazz makes me sing
and swing
but the blues
is my muse

Jazz grabs me
by the collar and
makes me holler

It spins me around
beating in my bones
like a heart full of sound

Jazz hypnotizes me
with its *blooblop*
deblee blooblop deblam

Ooh weee, that *blooblop*
deblee blooblop
deblam

The blues celebrates
the bruised with
sad stories and
funny-sounding news

It makes me think
about my sadness
and how I ain't alone

Yeah, it makes me
think about my sadness
and how I ain't alone

The blues makes me feel
a whole lot better
it hits my heart in
the funny bone

Poetry Means
the World to Me

Poetry means the world to me
it's how I laugh and sing
how I cry and ask why

Poetry comforts me
when I use jazz or
the blues or the way
regular folks talk—
the language
they use

Words don't always
have to be neat
and polished
like a statue

They should be
used used used
to say what you like
    or don't like
what you see think
or feel—

Words to fight against
hate and unnecessary
        suffering

Poetry is what *I* use
to say
        I love you

A Bag of
Oranges

A bag of oranges is
what she brings me

With a great big dimply grin
sweet as a Georgia peach
come to see *me* on my death bed

With her hand outstretched,
palm up, orange big and bright as the sun
as if death to her is a new day
      she brings the sun!

That child
makes the pain of my illness
go away
         this day!

Dear sweet Alice Walker
one of my favorite young writers
brings me a bag of oranges

Brings me oranges like
         a bag of sun

Sometimes Life
Ain't Always a Hoot

Sometimes life ain't
always a hoot
or a holler

But if you manage
to give it
a bother

Even if you miss
your mother
or don't like
your father

There'll be better days
up ahead

A whole mess of
happenin' days
up ahead

You can sit and sulk
suck your teeth
and sigh

Or love and laugh
and live life
by and by

Little Boy Blues

James Langston Hughes, known throughout his life as Langston Hughes, was born on February 1, 1902, in Joplin, Missouri, to Carrie Langston Hughes and James Nathaniel Hughes. Langston had a lonely childhood. His parents separated when he was one year old. His father moved to Mexico, where he went into the mining business, while his mother, who was trained to teach kindergarten and primary school, moved from place to place trying to find work. Langston occasionally lived with his mother but primarily lived in Lawrence, Kansas, with his maternal grandmother, Mary Langston. His grandmother was in her seventies, and when she wasn't telling Langston stories, she did not interact with him much. She didn't allow him to go out and play because she was concerned he would be harmed by the neighborhood white children, who sometimes chased him and called him racist names.

Grandma's Stories

Langston's grandmother's full name was Mary Patterson Leary Langston. She was raised free, though at the age of nineteen she escaped an attempt to kidnap her into slavery. She went on to become an abolitionist, working to abolish slavery. As a conductor for the Underground Railroad, she helped slaves escape to the North. Her first husband, Lewis Sheridan Leary, was an abolitionist too. He joined John Brown, a white preacher who fought against slavery, in an attack against a U.S. armory at Harpers Ferry, West Virginia, on October 16, 1859. Lewis Sheridan Leary was killed in the battle, and Mary Langston kept his blood-stained shawl, which was riddled with bullet holes. When Langston was a child she would sit him on her lap wrapped in this shawl and tell him these real-life stories. Langston never forgot her stories, and years later he wrote about them in the poem "Aunt Sue's Stories," the model for this poem. Langston lived with his grandmother until she died in 1915, when he was thirteen years old.

First Grade

When Langston was a child, schools were segregated and students were separated according to race. In 1907, when Langston was entering the first grade in Topeka, Kansas, the principal at the local all-white school told Langston's mother that Langston could not attend because he was black. She challenged this decision by appealing to the school board, saying that Langston was too young to walk to the black school, which was quite far away. She was successful in her appeal, and Langston was allowed to attend the all-white school. However, his first grade teacher took out her racist attitudes on Langston. She sat him in a corner in the last row. She called him hurtful names and made racist comments in front of the other students. Once she told a student who was eating licorice that the candy would turn him black like Langston. Langston remembered all the students turning around and staring at him. He tried to hide his feelings by keeping quiet and smiling. The teacher's actions affected the white students as well. Some students chased him after school, calling him names and throwing rocks, sticks, and bottles at him. Even though Langston learned about the cruelties of racism at a young age, he also learned that not all white people thought the same way. Some white teachers were nice to him and some white students stood up for him against his attackers.

Jim Crow Row

Langston learned from his grandmother and mother to stand up for what he knew was right. In 1914, when Langston was in the seventh grade, his teacher made all the black children sit in one row. Langston thought this segregation was unfair, so he made signs that read "Jim Crow Row" to protest. Jim Crow was the name of the laws that legalized segregation. When the teacher tried to remove the signs, Langston ran into the school yard shouting that the teacher had a Jim Crow row. He was expelled from school until parents joined the students in a demonstration against the teacher's racist practices. As a result of their protest, Langston was allowed back in school and the teacher was made to integrate the seating, allowing children of different races to sit together.

Libraries

When Langston was a small child, he would often go with his mother to the library. Books, stories, and poetry fascinated him from a very young age. After his grandmother died, he continued to spend his time in libraries when he went to live with his mother, his stepfather, Homer Clark, and his stepbrother, Gwyn. Throughout Langston's childhood and teenage years, books kept him company and comforted him during his times of loneliness and isolation.

In High School

Langston went to Central High School in Cleveland, Ohio. Even though this school was predominantly white, for the first time Langston felt at home. He made friends with other children his age who were mostly immigrants from Europe, which helped make up for his lonely childhood. His friends called him Lang, and he was a popular student who was involved in many activities. Langston graduated with honors in 1920, but his high school years were also filled with big decisions and hardships. In the summer of 1918, at the age of sixteen, Langston went to visit his mother in Chicago. He worked that summer to help his mother pay bills, but when it was time to leave, she wanted Langston to quit school, stay in Chicago, and continue to work to help her. She was filled with resentment at not being able to follow her own dreams. Consequently, she did not support Langston's goal to be a poet, and she didn't want him to go to college. But Langston did not want to end up like many of his high school friends, who left school only to find themselves trapped in dead-end factory jobs. He decided to stay in high school in Cleveland, where he had to support himself. He rented an attic room and lived on a diet of hot dogs and rice and the occasional free meal at a friend's house.

I Do Not Like My Father Much

Langston and his father were practically strangers. They had no contact from the time Langston was five until he was seventeen. Then, in 1919, his father sent for Langston to visit him in Mexico. Langston was excited about spending time with his father, but almost as soon as he met him, he was upset by his father's intense demeanor and mean temperament. His father was angry and bitter because of racism and poverty. But instead of understanding these problems, he blamed black people and poor people for the conditions in which they found themselves. Langston was shocked by his father's attitude and beliefs. He was also upset that his father, who was wealthy, was so stingy with his money. During a second visit with his father in 1920, after Langston graduated from high school, his father tried to convince him to go to college, become an engineer, and help him with his mining business. He wanted Langston to study in Switzerland, but Langston had his heart set on going to Harlem and being a poet. Langston finally convinced his father to send him to Columbia University, in Harlem, where he went a year later, in 1921. After a year Langston could not take the isolation of Columbia's campus or the math and engineering classes that took away from his writing, so he wrote to his father to inform him that he was leaving Columbia to pursue his dream of becoming a poet. Langston's father refused to support his dream, and he never sent Langston another letter.

Leaving Harlem for Africa

When Langston moved to New York City, he wanted to spend his time soaking up life in Harlem and the rest of the city where theater and art were centered. Langston's reputation as an emerging poet was growing, and this was the first time he had a chance to meet and befriend important writers and artists who knew him from his poetry which had been published in major black journals and periodicals. After dropping out of Columbia, Langston decided to seek adventure through travel. At the age of twenty-one, he boarded a ship, the *West Hesseltine*, which set sail for Africa on June 13, 1923. Langston got a job working on the ship so he could travel for free. It was during this initial journey to Africa that he decided to learn about the world, not through books but through travel, meeting new people, and learning about different cultures. He threw his books, which were primarily school books and books he had read as a child, overboard. But Langston kept one book, *Leaves of Grass*, a collection of poetry by Walt Whitman, his favorite poet.

All My Life

Throughout his adult life Langston traveled in search of firsthand knowledge and adventure. His first trip was to Africa and then to Paris, France. Later, when he had become an established writer, Langston was asked to participate in the making of a film in Russia. He also traveled to China, Japan, Cuba, Haiti, and other parts of the world, sharing his work with writers and making friends along the way. During his career, Langston was a great supporter of his peers as well as younger writers, and his extensive travels brought him into contact with writers from around the world. Spending time in Mexico with his father allowed Langston to learn Spanish. He went on to translate the works of many well-known Spanish-speaking writers, including the poetry of Federico García Lorca of Spain, a novel by Haitian writer Jacques Roumain, and the poetry of Cuban writer Nicolás Guillén, whose work had been influenced by Langston's.

Harlem Is the Capital of My World

Harlem is a part of New York City stretching from the East River to the Hudson River in the upper part of Manhattan. In the 1900s black people began moving into the area from lower Manhattan in search of better living conditions and reasonable rents. Others moved there from the South and the Caribbean, seeking better opportunities. But it was difficult for black people to get jobs because Harlem had its share of racial problems. In the early 1920s Harlem became the center of the black world—the primary location for black cultural expression and white patronage. This was the era known as the Harlem Renaissance, a vibrant and vital period when black writers, artists, musicians, actors, and poets flourished. Langston first set foot in Harlem on September 4, 1921, at the age of nineteen. He lived in Harlem on and off throughout his life, and it was the place where he found inspiration for many of his works. In 1948 Langston moved to 20 East 127th Street and lived there for the rest of his life.

Jazz Makes Me Sing

Jazz and the blues were a great influence on Langston's work. He was one of the first American poets to experiment with these distinctly American musical forms created by black people. While Langston was living in France in 1923, he worked washing dishes at a club. He was swept away by the sounds of jazz and the blues, which inspired him to write poems in his head as he scrubbed. He heard jazz and the blues live at clubs and on the radio. The force of this exuberant music inspired him to create new poetic forms. He took the rhythms and sounds of jazz and incorporated that playfulness and spontaneity into the language of his poems. He also borrowed from the blues, a musical form that utilizes repetition and treats sad themes in humorous ways. He performed and recorded his poetry with legendary jazz musicians such as bassist Charles Mingus.

Poetry Means the World to Me

Poetry was the central passion of Langston's life. The poets Langston was drawn to wrote for the common everyday people who worked and struggled to get by, people like those he knew growing up. Poets Carl Sandburg and Walt Whitman, who used the speech patterns, rhythms, and language of the people, were great influences on him. Langston was one of the first American poets to successfully capture and use jazz, the blues, and common speech in his poems. He also celebrated people who normally were not written about—the poor, the working class, and people of the street. Langston used his poems to make people feel good about themselves and to criticize

society for its unfairness. In 1920 Langston's first published poem appeared in *Brownies Book*, a magazine for black children founded in New York in October 1919 by W. E. B. DuBois. In 1926 Langston published his first book of poetry, *The Weary Blues*. He went on to publish thirteen volumes of poetry, win the prestigious Spingarn Medal, and become recognized as a world-class poet.

A Bag of Oranges

As Langston got older, he was a big influence on and supporter of younger writers and poets. He published various anthologies which included the works of younger writers. One such writer was Alice Walker, who went on to become a famous author herself, especially after her novel *The Color Purple* was published. In 1967, before Langston died, Walker visited him when he had the flu. None of Langston's friends, family, or the public knew he was critically ill, for Langston led a very private life. When Alice Walker came to visit the ailing older writer, she brought him a bag of oranges. Langston, who considered Alice Walker one of the best younger writers he knew, was moved by the sweet gesture of this woman in her early twenties. Langston Hughes died on May 22, 1967, at the age of sixty-five.

Sometimes Life Ain't Always a Hoot

Langston lived an exciting life of ups and downs. As a black man who grew up in the early 1900s, he had to overcome many obstacles, including racism and poverty. And although he became a famous and important American writer, he struggled financially throughout his life. He also experienced immense hardship because of his political views. In the 1950s, when Langston was in his fifties and already an established writer, his livelihood was threatened by the inquisitions of Senator Joseph McCarthy. Many American artists, entertainers, and activists were blacklisted and unfairly accused of treason because of their political ideas and affiliations. Langston survived this challenge as he had survived his previous problems with loneliness, isolation, and racism. His great spirit, filled with optimism and hope, kept him focused and moving forward with his work. In his well-known poem "Mother to Son," the narrator, a mother, says to her son, "Life to me ain't been no crystal stair." Langston always felt that even though life can be difficult, one must always look on the bright side. Tomorrow may have its challenges, but it also promises to be new and different.